TODAY I LAY

A SPECIAL THANKS to the RU editorial team for tirelessly working to produce this product with me: Carolyn Curington, Joy Kingsbury, Kay Niederwerfer, Beth Wilson, Amanda Amster, and Benjamin Luedke.

Design and Layout: Jeremy N. Jones, and Jessica Poggemiller

REFORMERS UNANIMOUS INTERNATIONAL

PO Box 15732, Rockford, IL 61132
Visit our website at www.reformu.com.
Printed in Canada
Cover design by Jeremy N. Jones

       Curington, Steven B., 1965-2010
Today I Lay: Engaging the Power of His Resurrection.
Steven Curington.

ISBN 978-1-60461-623-1

TODAY I LAY

ENGAGING IN THE POWER OF HIS RESURRECTION

STEVEN B. CURINGTON

DEDICATION

This book is dedicated to my good friend and ministry partner, Steve Schupp. Steve has taught me, many times over, to just simply wait on the Lord. Everything that Steve has received from the Lord has come as a result of a patient wait. His willingness to humble himself in adversity and quieting wait for God to empower him has been a great example to me and our many staff and students everywhere.

Bro. Steve, you have been exactly what I needed. You were worth the wait.

TABLE OF CONTENTS

LOSE IT; HE'LL USE IT!

"**BUT WHAT THINGS WERE GAIN TO ME, THOSE I COUNTED LOSS FOR CHRIST.** Yea doubtless, and I count all things but loss for the excellency of the knowledge of Christ Jesus my Lord: for whom I have suffered the loss of all things, and do count them but dung, that I may win Christ, And be found in him, not having mine own righteousness, which is of the law, but that which is through the **faith of Christ**, the righteousness which is of God by faith: That I may know him, and the power of his resurrection, and the fellowship of his sufferings, being made conformable unto his death;" Philippians 3:7-10

Please read the verse to your left and this introduction before continuing to chapter one. This verse is the foundational truth upon which all other truths will build. It is integral to understanding the power of His resurrection.

The most significant display of God's power in the Bible is the resurrection of Jesus Christ from the dead. In my opinion everything else, including the creation of the world, the miracles of the Old and New Testaments, the power that we see still at work in our world today, pales in comparison to the miracle of that Resurrection Sunday morning. Every power that the enemy had was thrown into the battle to keep Jesus in the grave. But the grave could not hold Him! Up from the grave He arose!

That same power that brought Jesus back to life—the indwelling Holy Spirit of God (Romans 8:11)—lives inside every Christian. Yet, many believers continue to live powerless, defeated, fruitless, and frustrated lives. They are still in bondage to sinful attitudes and actions. They do not yield to the fruits of the Spirit during difficult circumstances. Why are God's children living below their calling and privileges? I believe it is because they have not grasped the teaching of Scripture on how they can engage His resurrection power in every aspect of their lives. In Philippians 3, Paul lays out for us the process by which we can come to know and experience that power.

In this passage, we see our position—IN Him. The word *in* means surrounded by the limits. My book, entitled <u>Umbrella Fella: Overcoming Sin Through the Power of IN</u>, is written on this subject of living IN Christ. As a result of my studies in writing that book I have learned that there is great theology in the prepositions of the New Testament! God used this preposition over 100 times in the New Testament in order to show us our exact positioning with Him, that is to say, IN Christ.

This passage also exposes the Power that allows us to live the victorious life. It is found in yielding to the faith of Christ, and the righteousness of God. Carefully notice that it is not *our* faith or *our* righteousness that we need. The focus is on Christ's faith, God's righteousness, not on our faith or righteousness.

At Reformers Unanimous, we work with many people who struggled in school while they were growing up. Many of them did not have parents who encouraged them to stay in school, do their work, and make good grades. Others were already using drugs or alcohol, which affected their academic performance. As a result, many schools have lowered the bar of our educational requirements. Our nation has gone through a "dumbing down" of sorts of our vocabulary system.

So, today we find that many people have difficulty understanding simple vocabulary words. I believe that is one of the reasons behind peoples perception for the need of multiple Bible translations. It's because people are always looking for a Bible that is easier to read.

But we do not need a new Bible. We just need to expand our vocabulary! I encourage students of the Bible to use a dictionary to define words they may not understand. The older the dictionary, the more accurate the definition will be. Using a dictionary, we can then dissect and define a verse or passage to help us understand what God is saying to us through His Word.

With that in mind, let's dissect and define our passage using our 1828 Noah Webster's Dictionary:

"But what things were gain (valuable) to me, those I counted loss (something that yields a negative effect)…" –Philippians 3:7

Paul is claiming that everything that used to be valuable to him has now become a negative effect. Notice he does not see his prior values as neutral, but rather as *negative* impressions on his spiritual walk.

Verse 8 continues, "Yea doubtless, and I count all things but loss for the *excellency* (that means a pure heart) of the *knowledge* of Christ Jesus my Lord." This is not referring to knowledge <u>about</u> Christ, but the knowledge <u>of</u> Christ. It is referring to my personal relationship with Him.

Developing this personal relationship with Christ is our goal as believers. This is God's purpose and plan for us. His design for our lives is that we will reach the point where we move past information about Him to a personal relation with Him. This is not about acquiring historical information, but rather having a personal, intimate relation with someone we can know on a deep level. The end result of having this intimate relationship with Jesus Christ is excellency! That is to say, an intimate relationship with Christ develops a pure heart within us.

Now, the word *heart* gets used in a lot of different ways. Some people believe the heart refers to the mind or the intellect (we know "as a man thinks in his heart, so is he"). Others equate it with the emotions (we know that "out of the abundance of the heart the mouth speaketh"). We even use the heart as our symbol on Valentine's Day. Still others connect it to our will. We know that God hardened Pharaoh's heart. This was a manifestation of Pharaoh's stubborn will.

Indeed, we know it is true that the heart is influenced by all three portions of our soul—the mind, the emotions, and the will. But the heart is really a trigger system. Though it can be "flipped" to submit to the soul or spirit, the heart will determine how we will live. If it is under the influence of the Spirit of the Lord Jesus Christ, then we will walk after the Spirit. If it is under the influence of the flesh, then we will walk after our flesh.

The heart is probably the single most important facet of the Christian life. Scripture tells us, "Keep thy heart with all diligence, for out of it are the issues of life" (Proverbs 4:23). Because of this, Paul is saying in the Philippians 3 text that the things which were once valuable to him had become detrimental. The reason why they were so detrimental to him is because they negatively influenced his heart by captivating his meditations and thus hindering his personal relation with Jesus Christ.

He wanted not just an intimate personal relationship with Christ, but the pure meditations of heart that are a result of a personal relationship with Him. Now, let's look at the rest of what Paul had to say, and then after I dissect and define this passage I will explain what the Bible teaches it takes to build this kind of intimate relationship with Him.

"for whom I have suffered the loss of all things,"— *Paul had lost all of his "things"*

"and do count them but dung,"—*and he views those former things as animal excrement*

"that I may win Christ,"—*so that I can attain a personal relationship with Christ*

"and be found in him,"— *"so I can be surrounded by His influence"*

"not having my own righteousness, which is of the law,"—*that's self-righteousness, when man does the work*

"but that which is through the faith of Christ,"— *His (God's) measure of confidence in Himself*

"the righteousness which is of God by faith:"— *Holy Spirit empowered righteousness*

"that I may know him"—*that I may enjoy a deep, personal relationship with Christ*

"and the power of his resurrection,"—*His power on*

my new life

"and the fellowship"—*intimate familiarity that comes a result*

"of his suffering"—*the God-ordained adversity in life*
"being made"—*produced*

"conformable"—*a molding image*

"to his death."—*His suffering for the sake of others*
—Philippians 3:8b-10

Dissected, defined and paraphrased by me Paul is saying that he has suffered through the loss of all his things but has realized now that they are of no real value compared to the purer meditations he received as a result of his personal relationship with Christ. This realization drove Paul to develop a true Righteousness rather than a self developed righteousness. This drive propelled Paul to be willing to suffer great adversity so that he could experience an intimate affiliation with Christ's suffering and subsequently be endued with power from on high.

To be made conformable to the image of

his Son means to personally experience the crucified Christian life. To experience the crucified Christian life, there are two things for which we must be willing to suffer. First, we have to be willing to suffer for the *sins* of others. Second, we must be willing to suffer for the *sake* of others. It is hard enough to suffer for the sins of others when someone else's mistake brings us pain and heartbreak. But suffering for the sake of others requires a truly sacrificial spirit.

That is the pattern that Jesus Christ set for us. "For even hereunto were ye called: because Christ also suffered for us, leaving us an example, that ye should follow his steps:" (I Peter 2:21). We often hear people ask "WWJD—What Would Jesus Do?" The answer to that question is given to us in Scripture…He suffered! If we are going to enjoy intimate familiarity and fellowship with Him, we must be willing to follow Him, even to our own metaphorical cross in order that we might suffer for the *sins* and for the *sake* of others!

Note that this passage of Scripture promises us both great power and great adversity. How do we experience God's great power in the midst of great adversity? We *experience* that great power by being willing to lose everything we do not need! We *enjoy* that power by being willing to devalue everything we keep, and we *exercise* that power by being willing to suffer as our Savior suffered that we may forever relate to Him in a personal and intimate way. Please allow me to share God's wonderful plan for me, with you.

CHAPTER ONE

A PERSONAL RELATION BRINGS A PURER MEDITATION

PAUL COVETED THE PURE MEDITATIONS THAT COME AS A RESULT OF DEVELOPING A PERSONAL RELATION WITH CHRIST. Many Christians struggle with negative, critical, pessimistic, and competitive meditations. When we dwell on these things, it is obvious that we do not have the personal relationship with Jesus that He intends for us to have. Often we get our steps backward. We think that we need a purer meditator in order to enjoy a personal relationship. That is self-righteousness! Self-righteousness requires that we first do the work in our own power. Then, God will meet you halfway. No! The truth is that our personal relation must precede your purer meditations!

I experienced this in my own life. For years, I had a meditator that was critical, negative, pessimistic, and competitive. No matter what God did for me, I found fault. No matter what others did for me, I found fault in them. Whenever anyone did anything, I viewed them as having a personal agenda and quickly found flaw!

Yet, I wished I could do right. I wanted to live a life that was pleasing to God. I wanted to have a good family and a dynamic relationship with my wife. I desperately wanted God's power on my life. So, I sought and strove to have a deep, abiding relationship with Jesus Christ. In His mercy, despite my pessimistic attitude, God gave me an acceptable personal relationship with Him. But little did I know this slowly developing relationship would begin to heal my broken meditator.

I did not have to first muster my own willpower in order to overcome my negativity before I could enter into an intimate personal relationship with Jesus. I did not have to change my heart first—I had to change my relationship first, and then my heart was broken and changed.

I remember watching my pastor and wondering how it was possible for him to be so calm in the face of adversity. He had a peace that I did not have. What I eventually learned was that because of the intimate, personal relationship he had with Jesus, God had granted him a purer meditator. He had the ability to think Philippians 4:8 thoughts; and as a result, he was able to speak Philippians 4:8 words, regardless of how difficult his circumstances appeared.

A purer meditator grants us the ability to think balanced in the midst of any and all adversity. That is the goal that Paul laid out, and that we should be pursuing—to gain the excellency (or the pure heart) that comes from a dynamic, intimate, personal relationship with the Lord Jesus Christ.

Note that Paul calls Jesus the Lord. *Lord* is a title that indicates ruling authority. He calls Him "Lord" while in the context of describing the close, personal relationship he was developing with Him. Before I served full-time in the RU ministry, I had my training in the business world. Back then, I learned that we were not supposed to get too close to our boss. A subordinate-employer relationship is inherently unequal and equally unwise.

It is difficult to be in a close relationship with the person in authority over us. That kind of relationship makes it difficult for them to properly rule. *Rule* is an Old English word for our modern English word lead. It is hard to lead someone with whom we have a close relationship. The Bible tells us that we not only should be under the authority of Jesus Christ as our Lord, but at the same time, we may have an intimate personal relationship with Him. How do we do it? The Bible gives us an indication in our text of the level of sacrifice that we will have to make in order to obtain this pure meditation toward our ruling authority. The only real way to have a personal relationship with someone over us is for that person to be perfect! Our Lord *is* perfect!

A) Our Gain Cannot Remain

Before we experience a purer meditation, we will have to change what we value—"But what things were gain to me, those I counted loss for Christ (Philippians 3:7a). Now note that this does not necessarily mean that we will have to *give up* every gain we have retained. That may need to happen, but it is not usually the process. What does have to happen is that we must stop *counting* the things we have as *valuable*. We must lose the value that we attach to our gains and place that value on Him in order to know Christ.

Many of us look at financial prosperity as a goal in life. Yet, the Bible teaches that anything above sufficiency is too much to win Christ. That does not mean we cannot have more sufficiency. It means our *goal* should be simple sufficiency, and sufficiency will bring us contentment. The Apostle Paul said, "And having food and raiment, let us be therewith content" (I Timothy 6:8).

Paul also said, "My God shall supply all your need according to his riches in glory by Christ Jesus" (Philippians 4:19). When we do not have a personal relationship with Jesus Christ, we separate ourselves from *His* ability to supply all our needs. As we begin to gain things in our own power, we then attach our hearts to them. These self absorbing gains will then hinder not only our relationship with Jesus, but disqualify us for the purer meditations of our heart that would be the result of that relationship.

Paul realized that the things that had once been gains had become a hindrance to him. Again, that does not mean we cannot have things of value; **it means that they cannot have us!** We must never over indulge our appetites for personal gain, because if we do, they will harm and hinder our walk with God.

Satan will use any number of things to manipulate what we value in life. It could be the size of our bank account or the size of our house. It could be the clothing in our wardrobe or coveting the corner office. But whatever, apart from God Himself, is of great gain to us cannot remain. We must come to the position where we say, "I count my valuable things as a hindrance."

One of the great missionary inspirations of the past century was William Borden, often called Borden of Yale. His family was fabulously wealthy; and as a graduation present, they sent him on a trip around the world. While he traveled, God broke his heart for the mission field, and Borden returned home, not to take over the family business, but to go to Yale to prepare for a life of service as a missionary.

Borden turned his back on a fortune, and many of his friends thought he was wasting his life by planning to go to the mission field. In his journal, Borden wrote, "Say no to self and yes to Jesus every time." As a freshman at Yale, he started a campus prayer meeting that led to a revival breaking out. By the time Borden was a senior, it is said that 1000 of the 1300 students had been saved and were taking part in one of the many prayer groups that had sprung up at the school.

Feeling the call of God to reach the Muslim world, Borden went to Egypt after graduating from seminary so he could learn Arabic. He was just twenty-five when he contracted meningitis and died. Though some regarded his life as wasted, hundreds of young men were inspired by his story to follow him to the mission field. In the back of

his Bible, which was returned to his parents after his death, Borden had written these words:
NO RESERVES: NO RETREATS: NO REGRETS

Lord, let it be the same for me. How about you? RU IN?

B) Preferences Must Lose Their Appeal

Paul goes on to say that he counted "all things" as loss. Now this is not a repetition of his earlier point, but something different. In addition to counting those things that had once been valuable to him as a hindrance, Paul also says that there are some things that may not be great gain but do bring great pleasure. These have to be counted as loss, too.

He is referring to things that are important to us—our conveniences, preferences, hobbies, and habits. Some of us have many preferences in life that have no great value to others but are nevertheless extremely appealing to us. We want things to be done the way we prefer them to be done. This philosophy can sometimes negatively influence our walk with God, as well.

Everything must be surrendered. Not sold, just surrendered! Anything that has an inappropriate value or is unnecessarily appealing to us can hurt our walk with God. If we long for that intimate relationship, there is no room for anything else if its influence over us draws us away from Him.

Note that we are not talking about bad things. It is not wrong to have hobbies or to have preferences for the way things should be done. But, we must realize that those things can potentially compete for our affections, this will hamper or even destroy our walk with God. There are people for whom the breaking point is a Lazy Boy and a Diet Coke on non-church nights. They are not willing to give up these small privileges and instead, they are willing to tank their walk with God before they will sacrifice the slightest pleasure or preference.

Stuart Hamblen was a famous actor on the radio and in the movies in the 1930s and 1940s. Though he had grown up in a preacher's home, Stuart had left God far behind for the allure of Hollywood. But after attending a prayer meeting in 1949, he gave his life completely to God. He turned his back on fame and fortune and went on to become a noted Christian musician and speaker. In his song "Until Then" he wrote these lines:

The things of earth will dim and lose their value
If we recall they're borrowed for a while;
And things of earth that cause the heart to tremble,
Remembered there will only bring a smile.

C) Lose It and He Will Use It

Paul is not suggesting losing everything in the sense of complete abandonment. He is not talking about taking a vow of poverty. He simply means that we must give what we have to God. Everything that is ours has to become His. Now it is easy to say that everything we have is God's; but what if, like Job, we lost it? How would we feel then? Would we complain? If it is not ours, what right would we have to complain? If we complain over the loss of anything, then it is not His; it is ours!

Paul was willing to lose everything he had in

exchange for a personal relation that gave him a purer meditation. He did not hold on to anything from his former life. All of the gains and glories that were rightfully his were laid at the cross for the Lord. And by the way, Paul thought that was a pretty good trade!

Notice the single compelling reason Paul was willing to lose ownership of everything—"that I might win Christ." He would not value anything that would hinder his relationship with Jesus. Paul was willing to lose it that He might use it. He realized that the resurrection power of the Holy Spirit was available only if he surrendered everything to God's ownership.

I have prayed this prayer in my own life: "Lord, is this thing in my life having a negative effect on me? If it is hindering my walk with You, then I will turn it over to You to do with as you see fit." Sometimes, God has taken those things away. At other times, He has allowed me to keep them. But either way, He always generously removed my intense attachment to them in the process.

D) It Must Lose You, so You Can Win Him

Paul counted, or numbered, these things as dung so that he could win, or attain, Christ. Winning Christ is not referring to our gaining justification from God through belief in the sacrificial death of His Son. His desire to "win Him" is referring to the personal relation available to anyone who has experienced justification.

It is one thing to not have things of value; it is another thing not to seek them at all. Some people who have almost *nothing* are consumed by the thought of things; others who oversee much may hold his belongings lightly for the sake of their Lord, their Master. How do we look at our possessions? Paul counted them as dung. Paul most certainly would have had quite a few possessions before his conversion. To serve God, it must have required some legitimate downsizing for Paul.

He had been educated by Gamaliel, one of the greatest teachers of his day. Paul was from Tarsus, which is in modern-day Turkey. For his parents to have been able to send Paul such a distance to such a prestigious school, they would have had to have been very well off. He spoke multiple languages and was not just a subject, but a free-born citizen of the Roman Empire—a fairly rare distinction for a Jew.

In the transition from being a persecutor of the church who murdered and jailed believers, to being one of the most powerfully used men in the history of the church, Paul must have left some things behind. The things that had once mattered to Paul no longer had value to him. He changed his method of *evaluation* to reflect his new desire for a purer *meditation*.

If I asked you how much money was in your bank account, you would probably be able to tell me fairly accurately. That is because we count our money. We usually count the things that are valuable to us; and anything that attacks those things of value, we consider a negative effect. But yet, we seldom carefully count the things that improve our personal relationship with Christ, nor do we fear the things that hinder it. The reason is not because we have things, but because those things have us.

A purer meditation is wonderful, but it does not come without a cost. It comes only when we recognize anything that hinders our walk with God as negative. There was a man who had been a huge gambler before he was saved. He had risked and lost everything he owned and more on football games. After his conversion, he refused to watch football; it was a negative influence on his relationship. I am not saying that giving up football is required for everyone, but if that is what was keeping me from an intimate relationship with Jesus Christ, I would surrender it in a second! He is worth any sacrifice.

Paul is telling us that in order to have the power of the Holy Spirit, we must first establish a personal relationship with Him. In order to establish that relationship, we have to experience the resurrection. In order to experience the resurrection, we must first experience the crucifixion. The crucifixion for a believer is an obligation to crucify our affections and lusts. As Dr. Lester Roloff used to say, "Nobody ever got resurrected who wasn't dead first."

Many good Christians have a misguided

concept of crucifixion. We think it means we have to stop everything. The Christian life is not a stop sign. The secret to godly living is not, "Stop that!" The Christian life is a yield sign. When God says that something must die in our lives, we must be willing to sacrifice it for Him. Often people are so busy stopping things that they never learn to yield to the One Who calls us to a crucifixion.

CHAPTER TWO
TODAY I DIE

"THAT I MAY KNOW HIM AND THE POWER OF HIS RESURRECTION, AND THE FELLOWSHIP OF HIS SUFFERING, BEING MADE CONFORMABLE UNTO HIS DEATH" (Philippians 3:10). Notice the progression: Paul talks about knowing Jesus, then he talks about the resurrection, then he talks about the suffering; and finally, he talks about the crucifixion. Why did Paul place things in that order? Why end with the crucifixion? That was not the last event in the series of things that happened to Jesus; it was the first! Paul is talking about a process of events in an inverted order. In other words, to know any of these things, we must first know that precedes it in order.

We cannot know Him without going through each step in the right order. Many believers never get past the crucifixion. We often accept the crucifixion yet we never progress from there. We fail to become familiar with His suffering. Thus we never resurrect in newness of life. As a result of these failures, we never truly grow to know Him.

I describe it this way: we fail to turn our crucifixion into a resurrection. We have died to the old life, but we do not develop the new life that replaces it. Yes we are buried with Him by baptism into death but ought we not also be raised to walk in newness of life?

People "whose things have them" cannot enjoy this process. We must count them a loss if they have become a disruptive gain. That is the first step on the path to a personal relationship with Jesus Christ.

Knowing Jesus requires that we experience the great power that only comes through a resurrection. But we cannot be resurrected unless we have spent time in the tomb, developing that intimate familiarity with Jesus. To have all that, we must first be conformed to His death, our own personal crucifixion of self.

A) Molding into a Daily Dying Person

Notice that Paul did not say, "being conformed to his death." Instead, by inspiration, he wrote, "being <u>made conformable</u> unto his death." This is not a process we want to do; it is something He *makes* us do. It is not easy for our lives to lose its value to us.

One of the great missionaries in history was Jonathan Goforth. He worked for decades in China and saw thousands of converts come to Christ. Once, he and his wife, Rosalind, went on a trip to visit some of the churches they had started. When they returned to their mission compound, they found that someone had broken into their home and stolen almost all of their possessions. Rosalind wrote that she was devastated, but her husband turned to her and said, "Rosalind, they were just things." That is the attitude of a daily dying person.

Nothing—that means no *thing* and no

person—will get in the way of a daily dying person searching for intimacy with Christ. Their life's drive is to have nothing between their soul and their Savior!

When God asks us to sacrifice something of self in any way, we often struggle to willingly conform. But, He will *make* us conform to the image of Christ's death, and we must allow Him to do so if we are to enjoy the intimate fellowship with Him that transforms our hearts. This is not a one time process. . . it must continue day after day. As, Paul proclaimed, "I die daily" (Galatians 2:20). So we too must be willing to die in order to reach this level of intimacy with Christ.

It is important to remember that Jesus did not die to pay for His sin. He was the holy, innocent, spotless Lamb of God. He died for the sins of others. It is not as difficult for us to be willing to face up to the consequences for our own actions. (That does not mean it is easy, just that it is easier than suffering for the actions of others.) In our own crucifixion, we must learn to relate to a suffering, not just for the sins of others, but also for the sake of others. That is the daily death to which we must be molded.

Unfortunately, many believers reject this sacrificial step. We are less willing to suffer for the sins of others, or for the sake of others versus suffering for our own mistakes. As a result, we miss out on the glorious resurrection power and the intimate fellowship with Jesus that is the key to true victorious living.

Many churches struggle to get their members involved in the ministry. Why would pastors have to plead for Christians to promote the gospel? Why are so many believers only interested in what they can receive from Christ, without being willing to give what Christ requests in return? Simply put, it is because we refuse to be molded into a daily dying believer. We want to receive the benefits of our salvation, but we are not willing to take up our cross and follow the "Via Del a Rosa"—the Way called Suffering!

We will never experience an intimate relationship with Him until we are willing to put up with many inconveniences for the sake of others.

When the pastor asks for someone to help with a ministry, and we feel an inward persuasion that we should help, where do you think that persuasion is coming from? Do you think it is the devil? Well, then pray tell by process of elimination, who is it? It is the Holy Spirit of God, moving us to live as Jesus did—for the sake of others.

So many times we experience outside pressure from God-ordained authority and internal persuasion of the Holy Spirit, but we still do not respond. It is because a response would require a sacrifice. Yet, it is that suffering sacrifice that we must experience in order to have an intimate familiarity with Christ.

Good things—recliners, the football games, the 24-hour news channel, hobbies—can all get in the way and keep us from knowing Jesus, but only *if* we are not willing to give them up when God prompts us to sacrifice self for the sake of others. Again, this is not a natural process. It requires being conformed, as Paul said "being made conformable," and God is able to either make us or break us if we are not willing to yield to Him and become daily dying people.

We are not naturally prone to be poured into a mold of self-sacrifice. One thing I learned very quickly when we started Reformers Unanimous is that people do not mess up their personal lives between 8 a.m. and 5 p.m. No, they blow it between 8 p.m. and 5 a.m.! The problems people have and the struggles they face do not fit inside of a convenient business day. When people sin, they will soon call for help. Sometimes we have to get out of bed to come to the rescue. We will never be willing to do such a thing unless we have concluded that God wants us to suffer for the sins or sake of another. It is not natural; it is supernatural! It happens only as we yield to the internal persuasion of the Spirit.

B) Gains Must Be Replaced with Pains

Not only do the things that once were valuable to us need to be surrendered to His control, but as we enter into the fellowship of His death, we must be willing to experience great pain. Remember the story of the three Hebrew children. Shadrach,

Meshach, and Abednego were commanded to bow down to the idol that Nebuchadnezzar had built. They refused. Now they did everything absolutely right. They resisted the temptation to take the easy road. They did so even under great pressure and threats.

They were committed to doing right regardless of their adversity. Did things get better because they handled the situation in a godly manner? No; in fact, it got worse! When you make the commitment to reach out, sacrificing yourself for the needs of others, the road is not going to be smooth. So many people are surprised when things go wrong. But Peter said, "Beloved, think it not strange concerning the fiery trial which is to try you, as though some thing happened unto you:" (I Peter 4:12). In other words, you should expect it; *stranger* things have happened!

Paul experienced this is his own life. He had been greatly empowered to preach the Gospel effectively. He had seen numerous churches established and people saved. He had been given visions from God that no one else had. But he also suffered greatly because of it.

Second Corinthians 12:7-10 "And **lest I should be exalted above measure** through the abundance of the revelations, there was given to me a thorn in the flesh, the messenger of Satan to buffet me, **lest I should be exalted above measure**. For this thing I besought the Lord thrice, that it might depart from me. And he said unto me, My grace is sufficient for thee: for **my strength is made perfect in weakness**. Most gladly therefore will I rather glory in my infirmities, **that the power of Christ may rest upon me**. Therefore **I take pleasure** in infirmities, in reproaches, in necessities, in persecutions, in distresses **for Christ's sake**: for when I am weak, then am I strong."

Pay careful attention to what Paul is saying in this passage. His suffering was his "thorn in the flesh." It was given to him by God! It was for his own good. When Paul realized that God's grace was sufficient, he stopped fighting his suffering. Instead he said "I take pleasure" in those things that hindered me! Paul was willing to trade his natural strength for God's supernatural strength through suffering in order that he might enjoy intimate fellowship with Him.

I believe a lot of us spend much of our time in prayer asking God to take away the painful things in our life that He has given us! We expect our pain to be replaced with great gain. Instead, we find it replaced with more pain. That is the fellowship of His suffering. Jesus had to humble Himself to become a man, but He also had to humble Himself a second time to become obedient to the cross. Double humility seems unfair. It is not unfair; it is familiar!

Jesus earnestly prayed in the Garden for a way out. In fact, the Bible says His sweat was as great drops of blood. He asked His Father for the cup to pass from Him. Did the cup pass? Why not? Didn't the Father love the Son? Of course He did. But it was God's will—His purpose and His plan—that Jesus suffer. What Jesus experienced was God-ordained adversity.

I have some news for you today. God has some adversity planned for you. That adversity is not intended to drive you back into the world. Instead, it is meant to drive us deeper into our relationship with Jesus. That we might become familiar with one another. It is meant that we might rely on Him more than ever before. Through that suffering comes the intimate familiarity with Jesus.

If we pay attention as we read our New Testament, we will find some words that describe the apostles' response to their adversity, and they are words that do not seem to belong together. Next to words that indicate great pain, suffering, distress, and torture, we find words of joy and peace. Let me show you some examples of what I mean.

Paul said, "And I will **very gladly** spend and be spent for you; though the **more** abundantly I love you, the **less** I be loved" (II Corinthians 12:15). Paul gave everything he had for the Corinthians, and he did it gladly. Most people do not give anything gladly, let alone everything. Someone once said, "When it comes to giving till it hurts, most people have a low threshold of pain!"

Did the Corinthians appear to appreciate the

sacrifices that Paul had made for them? Did they return the love he showed to them? Not exactly! He said the more he loved them, the less they loved him in return. Why was Paul willing to do that? He was not receiving gratification or seeing success. It seems, the more he did, the worse things became. Yet, Paul continued on. He was fellowshipping with Christ. They were becoming familiar. When we sacrifice for the sake of others, we have something in common with Christ. It was not enough for Jesus to die on the cross. They had to stab Him with a spear too!

I learned quickly after starting Reformers Unanimous that if I was going to look for gratitude from our students for my inspiration, I was in real trouble. It seemed like some of those we helped the most, sacrificed for the most, and invested in the most, were the most ungrateful, troublesome, and rebellious students that we had. I had to run to Jesus just like Paul did.

Again Paul said, "Yea, and if I be offered upon the sacrifice and service of your faith, I joy, and rejoice with you all" (Philippians 2:17).

Paul not only had joy when he sacrificed for the Philippians, he had it again and again. That is what *rejoice* means—joy that repeats itself. As Paul's suffering and sacrifices were repeated, so was his joy. Instead of becoming weary and depressed by the pain, he became more joyful. In a holy way, suffering produces joy. If we yield to becoming a self-sacrificing, suffering saint, joy becomes a continuing, reinforcing cycle that repeats itself over and over again. Sound fun? If not, then it is not familiar. Some say, "try it; you'll like it!" Paul says, "die over it; you will like it."

This joy is possible because it does not come from us; it comes from Him! Paul said, "And ye became followers of us, and of the Lord, having received the word **in much affliction**, with **joy OF the Holy Ghost**" (I Thessalonians 1:6). The believers in Thessalonica had received the Word, but to get it, they had to endure affliction. In this case, the word "much" literally means "a multitude," and the word translated "affliction" is the same word Jesus used in talking about the Tribulation! It was not just a hangnail or a few worries. These believers suffered repeatedly and greatly. Yet, they had joy because their fellowship with Christ gave them the power of the Holy Spirit. And the Bible tells us that the fruit of the Spirit is . . . joy!

In Roman times, Christians suffered great persecution. They were tortured and killed by the droves. Many were taken to the great coliseums and slaughtered by wild animals for the entertainment of the crowds. Others were held in prison or dungeons for years. Yet, throughout all these sufferings, joy prevailed.

We looked at Paul praying to God about his thorn in the flesh. Some people identify Paul's thorn in the flesh as perhaps an eye problem or a physical ailment that he suffered as a result of his persecutions. Others think it was a habitual sin with which he struggled.

My pastor has a message on this passage that provided me with a new insight. Paul called his thorn in the flesh a "messenger of Satan." The word *messenger* appears some ninety times in our English Bible. In every one of those other cases, it is referring to a person. The Bible does not tell us what his messenger of Satan was, but it seems likely it was a *who*. Paul had **one person** who was a constant source of irritation and struggle in his life. He repeatedly prayed for God to take that person of pain away, but God refused.

Paul needed the thorn to keep him from being "exalted above measure." Paul, writing through the inspiration of the Holy Spirit, repeated that exact phrase twice. Why—because Paul was prone to pride. To humble him, God changed his name from Saul, which means "big head" to Paul, which means "little one." Then, God added a double dose of humility with a thorn in the flesh. It was for Paul's own good. Paul learned to glory in it—most gladly! Over time, he learned that pain was the thing that made him sing!

It was not that Paul enjoyed the pain. It hurt just as much after he accepted it through God's grace as it did before when he was praying for it to be removed. What had changed was Paul's *outlook* toward his sacrifice. He suffered *gladly* so that "the power of Christ may rest upon me."

Notice that he did not say the power was *on* him or in him. It was *upon* him. That literally means both *up* and *on*. If you fill a glass over the top with water, the water will rest **on** the glass. That cannot happen if the glass is only partly full. It has to be all the way full and overflowing. Then the water is both *up* the glass and *on* the glass. Paul was glad to endure great infirmities (or weaknesses) so that the power of Christ could fill him up until He was flowing out of his life.

It was not just Paul that felt this way about his call to suffer for the sins and sake of others. Earlier we looked at Peter's challenge for us to not be surprised when trials come. Remember what Peter wrote? "Beloved, think it not strange concerning the fiery trial which is to try you, as though some strange thing happened unto you: But **rejoice**, inasmuch as ye are **partakers of Christ's sufferings**; that, when his glory shall be revealed, ye may be **glad** also with exceeding joy" (I Peter 4:12-13). When we give Him our gains, He replaces it with pains; and we will enjoy the joy that comes with it. I promise that from that point forward, you will not want to live without it anymore.

Jesus said, "**Blessed** are ye, when men shall revile you, and persecute you, and shall say all manner of evil against you falsely, for my sake. **Rejoice**, and be exceeding **glad**: for great is your reward in heaven: for so persecuted they the prophets which were before you" (Matthew 5:11-12). When you sacrificially do things for the sins and the sake of others, you can expect to suffer. Be exceeding glad! Does this sound familiar? Why not?!

God knows we will suffer and that we will need His help. That is why Jesus sent the Comforter—He knew we were going to need the Holy Spirit to give us comfort in the midst of trials. God does not want or expect us to stay within our own comfort zone. He gives us His Comforter. A recliner is a mighty uncomfortable position for a man wearing a suit of armour! Someone needs to bring us comfort. But it's not me, it is He!

One of the brightest and most promising young preachers in the British Empire was John Patton. His church was growing rapidly, people were drawn to his clear preaching, and they saw his obvious love for others. People were shocked when he resigned his pulpit to reach the cannibals who lived in the New Hebrides Islands. Many thought he was throwing his life away as the cannibals had already killed and eaten at least one missionary who attempted to work among them.

Patton later recounted a conversation with one church member who argued that he should not go. "You will be eaten by the cannibals!" The man exclaimed. Patton replied, "confess to you, that if I can but live and die serving and honoring the Lord Jesus, it will make no difference to me whether I am eaten by cannibals or by worms."

After more than fifty years of fruitful ministry, John Patton died on Aniwa Island in 1909. In one of the churches that he founded, a plaque was placed in his honor. It reads:

"In memory of John Geddie Patton, D.D., born in Scotland, 1815, minister in Prince Edward Island seven years, Missionary sent from Nova Scotia to Aneiteum for twenty-four years. He landed in 1848, were no Christians here, and when he left in 1872 were no heathen."

C) Pain Must Become Our New Gain

When (and only when) we know the fellowship of His sufferings on a personal and intimate level, can we come to know the power of His resurrection. When we begin to experience unappreciated, or at least under appreciated, pain, we know that it is time to get up out of the tomb. We are ready to walk in the Spirit because we now have His resurrection power available to us.

Here is a pattern I have seen repeated many times. God begins to rip the cover off our weaknesses that He might expose them to us. To do this, He puts us through a trial of our faith. We suffer as He searches our heart through these trials. Often, we see that pain as something that is weighing us down and keeping us from the Lord, and we reject it. But as time passes, we eventually identify our problems and yield to the will and purpose of God.

In review, when we gain this position in Christ, those things that were former gains we should now consider a negative effect. As we trade our gains, we experience new pain. But, as we endure that pain in the proper spirit, that pain becomes our new gain. It creates an intimate fellowship, and that relationship prepares us for His power to resurrect within us.

But, sometimes, the pain is too much. We say, "This is hurting me, and I want it to stop!" Like Paul did, we beg the Lord to take it away. But unlike Paul, we are not willing to accept God's grace as sufficient. We begin to think negative, pessimistic thoughts. We say, "It's just not worth it." And we climb off the cross! As a result, we become ineffective for Christ. We must wait patiently for our death so that the pain can turn to gain. Then, in His time, we can experience His resurrection. There is no shortcut to this process. We cannot avoid it. We must die and be buried for a time before we can rise for His glory.

Only after experiencing His resurrection do we have His power to face our battles. Many of us face battles alone, relying on our own strength and power. It is no wonder that so many Christians are living defeated lives. If the archangel Michael needed God's power to defeat Satan (Jude 9), what on earth makes us think we can defeat the enemy on our own? Every battle we fight in His power brings victory; every battle we fight on our own brings eventual defeat.

This resurrection power is not a one time thing. Remember Paul said, "I die daily" (I Corinthians 15:31). If we reach a point at any time on any day where we are not willing to give up a gain or experience a pain, the resurrection power of the Spirit will be gone that fast! We will have to go back to the cross, or back in that tomb, and wait patiently to be resurrected again. The power of Christ cannot rest on a man who will not glory in his infirmities.

D) New Gains Break Chains

Yes, we know that our resurrection brings us new life. If we are willing to die every day, we will enjoy the benefit of being resurrected with regularity. This process provides us freedom from sinful dominations. Now, that does not mean we are free from the influence and presence of sin. I know some people teach that, and I wish they were right. It would be nice if all the influence of sin was taken away. But it is not! Rather, Paul taught, "For sin shall not have dominion over you: for ye are not under the law (where man does the work), but under grace (where God does the work)" (Romans 6:14). We no longer have to live under the power of sin anymore, but its presence is ever with us!

A deep relationship with Christ is the only thing that can effectually break sin's chains. Our will-power, self-control, and determination will not break the bonds of sin. Do you remember the story of the maniac of Gadera, in which many people had tried everything to control that man. He was homeless, violent, mean, self destructive and naked. He was a "nude dude in a rude mood!"

They had bound him with chains; but because of the demonic control in his life, he broke them and continued his wild ways. But just a few moments alone with Jesus was enough to change him completely. Before the chains could not keep him *from* sin; now, because of his new relationship, the chains of sin could not keep him *in* sin.

In John 8:32 Jesus said, "Ye shall know the truth (Jesus), and the truth (Jesus) shall make you free." When you come to know Jesus, then— and only then— will Jesus make you free. Your level of freedom is 100% dependent upon your personal relationship with Christ. It is not about information; it is about a personal relation. We can know all we want to know about God, but that does not make us free. It is only a personal relationship with God that makes us free.

We need to remember that our goal is to not only be found as Christians, but to take that second step after we are justified and begin to enjoy the benefits of our sanctification. We know that justification is a free gift of God; and in the same sense, sanctification is something that we have been given that needs to be unbound. The Bible says that Christ died to pay our payment for sin and death. Our penalty for sin was paid for us through our justification; but the power thereof was provided through our sanctification.

Many people enjoy the experience of

justification but fail to enjoy the benefits of their sanctification. When we are sanctified, we are set apart for sacred use. But this does not mean that we are always being used sacredly. All Christians are set apart. We are set apart at the moment of our salvation so that God can use us. But because of our selfish view of sanctification, God is unfortunately unable and, at times, unwilling to use us.

When we accept Jesus Christ and Him crucified, we are justified at that moment. However, to enjoy the benefits of our sanctification, we need to take the next step and develop an intimate, personal relationship with Him. Our justification is based on God knowing us; our sanctification is based on us knowing God.

Peter said, "But grow in grace, and in the knowledge of our Lord and Saviour Jesus Christ" (II Peter 3:18). That kind of spiritual growth comes only as a by-product of a personal relationship with Him. Many people are confused about their sanctification. I have had people ask me, "Brother Steve, is there some sort of a second blessing out there I should be seeking?"

Some people teach a doctrine whereby you accept Christ as your personal Savior; and then, after years of studying the Bible or patient waiting, we experience a double blessing, or a second dose of the Holy Spirit. No, that is not it at all. Implemented sanctification, what some people mistakenly call a second blessing, is not us getting more of the Holy Spirit; it is the Holy Spirit getting more of us.

When the great evangelist D. L. Moody was alive, he was known as a man who walked in the power of the Holy Spirit in an unusual way. Once a group of pastors was meeting to consider inviting Moody to come and preach a revival in their town. After listening to these men sing Moody's praises for awhile, one pastor got fed up. He said, "You men talk like Moody has a monopoly on God." One wise pastor responded, "No, God has a monopoly on Moody!" That is what implemented sanctification should look like in practice.

Sin dwelt within the soul of man after the fall for thousands of years. Man had little choice. He needed stark rules placed upon him to keep him from satisfying his appetites. He did have the benefits of an internal persuasion of the Holy Spirit to empower him to overcome the power of sin. But then, Christ died and was resurrected. For a believer, sin is then cast out of the soul and relegated to a position within the members of the body. Sin now dwells in our members (Romans 6), but no longer does it rule within our soul.

First John 3:9 confuses a lot of people. It states, "Whosoever is born of God doth not commit sin; for his seed remaineth in him: and he cannot sin, because he is born of God." Some people think that means Christians do not sin. I am here to tell you that they do! But, when we sin, it is the body (not the born again soul) that is sinning.

We do not *commit* sin in the soul; we *permit* sin in the soul. We *commit* sin in the body (Romans 7:17,20). We have the ability to yield to the Spirit and overcome sin's persuasive influence over the soul, but we often choose rather to yield to the sin that dwells in our body. Sin may have an overwhelming persuasive presence, but it does not have any real authority that we do not choose to give it. If we are trying to be righteous in our own power, and there are many believers doing that, we are living our Christian life as if we remain under the law (where man does the work). As a result sin will regularly defeat us. But, sin cannot automatically take control of us as children of God to do wrong. We only sin when we yield to its persistent influence.

Sin has control on believers who are not living in grace. Jesus said, "Ye shall know the truth, and the truth shall make you free." (John 8:32) Once again we need to grasp this principle firmly. It is the reason why so many Christians live defeated lives. Our freedom is dependent upon our knowing Jesus, the Truth. Without knowing Him, you may be found, but you will remain quite bound.

Maybe they sing this song at your church:

The things I used to do, I don't do them anymore
The things I used to do, I don't do them anymore
The things I used to do, I don't do them anymore
There's been a great change since I've been born again.

What I have found though is that a lot of people change the old "things" they used to do for a whole new set of "church-accepted" stubborn habits. They have just traded one set of addictions for another. Whether it is a critical spirit or negativity or apathy or laziness or covetousness, they are just as bound as people who are addicted to drugs or alcohol or pornography.

The only solution is to get on the cross with Jesus Christ. But if we are not willing to suffer, we will not go to our cross and become beneficial for others. Yes, God does love us just like we are (I wish I had a dollar for every time I have heard that one!); but He loves us too much to let us stay there. Until we know Him, we will never have the freedom that comes from knowing Him.

Too many Christians live as if just being saved gives them immediate power with God. No, it gives us access, but from there we need to harness that power through a clean transparent vessel.

If you remember the story of Lazarus, just being resurrected is not the end of His plan. Jesus went to the tomb and called out, "Lazarus, come forth!" Even though he had been dead four days, Lazarus came out of the tomb. However, he was still bound by the grave clothes, and he could not free himself. Jesus told the people to unbind Lazarus and let him go free.

The victorious, successful, rejoicing Christian life is not just about being saved; it is about walking freely in the Spirit. Only in His power can we love God and love others. We must be freed from our sinful habits and addictions. Romans tells us that He died unto sin once. We will not have to die to sin more than He did. However, though we will die only once for *sin* at salvation, we will die to *self* quite often in order to enjoy the benefits of implemented sanctification.

CHAPTER THREE
TODAY I LAY

IT HAS BEEN SAID THAT THE DAY BETWEEN GOOD FRIDAY AND RESURRECTION SUNDAY IS THE MOST BORING DAY IN AMERICA. We take the day off work for Good Friday and have great family fun time. As well, on Resurrection Sunday, many people will go to church to fulfill their religious obligations. Some of them are part of what is called the "Holly-Lily" bunch. They go to church on Christmas and Easter. But, there is a period of time between the remembrance of the crucifixion and the celebration of the resurrection. It is usually a day of rest or relaxation that can be quite boring. Surely, this must be a symbolic remembrance of something on this Saturday?!

In this chapter, I want to focus our attention

on the time we spend with Christ in the tomb. This is the day *we* lay.

Please understand this: The time we spend in the tomb is as vitally important to our walk with Him as our crucifixion and resurrection. We cannot overlook this process. It may not have the glamour of the resurrection or the gore of the cross, but it is only in the tomb that we develop our deep, abiding personal fellowship with Jesus Christ.

In Romans 6, Paul introduces us to a lifestyle characterized by victory and not defeat. It is the promise of a new life! The Bible says in Romans 6:3-4, "Know ye not, that so many of us as were baptized into Jesus Christ were baptized into his death? Therefore we are buried with him by baptism into death: that like as Christ was raised up from the dead by the glory of the Father, even so we also should walk in newness of life." Here we clearly see that we are to die *with* Christ, we are to be buried *with* Christ, and we are to be resurrected *with* Christ into newness of life.

Most Christians embrace the crucifixion

process taught in Chapter Two. We understand that we must regularly and willingly die to self. We often quickly boast to others how we die to this and sacrifice ourselves for that. May I say that, although we are committed to dying with Christ, we must also wait patiently in order to be resurrected with Him. There is no resurrection without a sacrifice, and there is no sacrifice without a death on the cross.

We all long for His great power on our life. I have heard people say things like, "If I would only be willing to die with Christ, or for Christ, or because of Christ, then I could experience this great new life." However, according to Philippians 3:10, the power of the new life is not found in the crucifixion, but it is found in the resurrection. It is only through the power of the resurrection that we can walk in newness of life.

Many Christians are willing to die to self, but that is just not sufficient enough. Those who believe it is sufficient will never learn to live in true victory. Instead, they will live a life of rejection. They will fail because while they may be rejecting the world, they are not accepting what Christ really has to offer. "For if we have been planted together in the likeness of his death, **we shall be also** in the likeness of his resurrection: Knowing this, that our old man is crucified **with him**, that the body of sin might be destroyed, that henceforth we should not serve sin. **For he that is dead is freed from sin**. Now if we be dead with Christ, we believe that **we shall also live with him**" (Romans 6:5-8). Hey, dead man, where is your new life? Where is your victory? Victory is found in a sequence of death, burial, and then resurrection!

As mentioned earlier, on Good Friday, we symbolically contemplate the death *of* Christ. On Easter Sunday, we celebrate the resurrection *of* Christ. But, if we died *with* Him on Good Friday, we should actually be contemplating our willingness to continually die *with* Him; that is to say, to daily die. Similarly, we celebrate the risen life of Christ on Easter Sunday. We should be considering if He is up from the tomb with or without me?!

Our failure to patiently wait for our

resurrection with Him is the reason why we fail to enjoy the newness of the Christian life? Why do we embrace the crucifixion and never experience our own personal, victorious resurrection? I believe our answer is that we *overlook* our time in the tomb. Hosea 6:1-3 says, "Come, and let us return unto the LORD: for he hath torn, and he will heal us; he hath smitten, and he will bind us up. **After two days will he revive us: in the third day** he will raise us up, and we shall live in his sight. Then shall we know, **if we follow on to know the LORD:** his going forth is prepared as the morning; and he shall come unto us as the rain, as the latter and former rain unto the earth."

Verse 1 is a picture of our crucifixion. But, what follows the crucifixion? Is it the resurrection? No! The crucifixion is followed by a time in the tomb: for today I lay! But after our time in the tomb, we will be revived. *Revive* means new life. Do you know what it takes to experience new life? It takes new death!

In this passage, Hosea is prophetically speaking about *our* death, burial, and resurrection with Jesus Christ. Remember that Christ's death, burial, and resurrection are the pattern we must follow in order to obtain our own Christ likeness, as well. Yes, this truth must be understood, comprehended, and assimilated into our own lives if we are to ever really experience the process of our very own DBR (Death, Burial, and Resurrection).

Notice the statement in verse one, "he hath torn." This indicates that God is the one who put Jesus (and us) through the crucifixion process. Our crucifixion is not just a one-time willingness to die to worldliness when we accept Jesus as our personal Savior. It is also our daily dying to self. Our daily death is a willingness to accept whatever God has for us, or what He does not want us to have, as well. This means we must reject our frustrations in the face of difficult circumstances and consistently crucify our fleshly wishes, wants, and worries.

This death comes through a tearing. Doesn't God love us? Then, why does He tear us? God tears us so that we may die to sin and live through Him! He puts us through painful situations so that we can live again. The construction of this statement tells us that this tearing is already an accomplished fact. God has allowed that burden, trial, or situation that we might die. But, we will never resurrect without first experiencing a crucifixion.

God has torn us, but He has also healed us. I am so glad God loves me enough to do both! Some people only emphasize the judgment of God while others only emphasize His love. Each approach misses the mark. God both tears and heals—and it is all for our benefit.

In Deuteronomy 32:29, God says, "I kill and I make alive, I wound and I heal." It is God who allows physical death, and it is also God who imputes upon us a spiritual death. Likewise, it is the same God who allows us to resurrect our souls. We can neither be crucified nor resurrected by ourselves. All of this is done **with** Christ by the power of His Spirit.

However, we must realize that whenever we experience the painful tearing of the crucifixion, the Lord Jesus Christ is going through it **with** us. We never suffer pain alone. Romans 6:6 says, "Knowing this, that our old man is crucified *with* him." When we are crucified, we are crucified with Christ. He suffers because we suffer! Galatians 2:20 says, "I am crucified *with* Christ: nevertheless I live; yet not I, but Christ liveth in me: and the life which I now live in the flesh I live by the faith **of** the Son of God, who loved me, and gave himself for me."

We often wish that we could have more faith. How many times I've heard someone say, "I could live a better Christian life if God would grant me more faith." We already have all the faith we could ever need! We have God's faith. I have heard of Christians who carry around a mustard seed to challenge themselves to build more faith. This is not necessary.

Let me give you the context of that teaching. In Luke 17:6, Jesus said, "If ye had faith as a grain of mustard seed, ye might say unto this sycamore tree, Be thou plucked up by the root, and be thou planted in the sea; and it should obey you" In Matthew 17:20, Jesus said that same mustard seed of faith could move a mountain. But that statement was not made in the abstract. This was

Jesus' response to the disciples' request to teach them how to increase their faith. What point was He making? He was teaching His disciples that we do not need more faith; rather, we need to use the faith God has already given to us. Only God can move mountains. That takes more faith than I have ever seen. Thus, we must conclude we only need a mustard seed of His faith in order to move mountains! If He wanted us to increase our own faith, then why would He have given us *His* fruit of the Spirit—faith?

We are commanded by God to love Him and others. Before I was saved, I knew how to love people. But my love for them was a flawed love. It was selfish love. God's love is unselfish, for it is perfect love. If, after my conversion, I looked to people and said, "I want to love you selfishly," that would be a waste of time. As a Christian, we ought to yield to God's unselfish love instead of our own self-love. In like manner, my joy before Christ was useless to Him. It is my joy since Christ came into my life that God would have me exercise in difficult circumstances. I had a measure of peace before I accepted Christ, but now I have this peace that passes understanding. It would be silly for me to rely on my imperfect peace when I can enjoy God's perfect peace.

Yet, when it comes to our faith, we often think that it is something we need to develop on our own. If my love is not sufficient to help people, if my own joy is not sufficient to remain calm in the face of adversity, and if my own peace is not going to help me through the storms of life; then likewise, my faith is not enough to help me live the crucified Christian life. I may need my own weak and simple faith to accept Christ, but I need His mountain-moving faith to accept death!

Again, we see I am crucified *with* Christ; I am not crucified by myself. I experience a crucifixion and a resurrection *with* Him. Romans 6:5 says, "For if we have been planted together in the likeness of his death, we shall be also in the likeness of his resurrection:" We are crucified together, and then we are planted together with Him in the tomb. And then, and only then, are we able to resurrect together with Him!

The Spirit-filled, Hidden Christian life can be represented by the use of a shoe. If I were to take my shoe off and say to it, "Come over here," that shoe would not move. (And if it did, I'd be moving faster!) However, if I put my foot **in** the shoe and I say to it, "Hey shoe, come over here," that shoe can go wherever I command it. But it is not the shoe; it is you *in* the shoe. Likewise, the Christian life is not you; it is Christ *in* you!

We can go where God wants us to go. We can do the difficult tasks that God wants us to do. However, we can only do these after we have experienced a crucifixion *with* Christ and an eventual resurrection *in* Christ. We must experience the light of the resurrection, *before* we can walk in the light as He is in the light (I John 1:9). It is then that we will see the great joy in sacrificing for the Lord.

In Romans 6, 7, and 8, Paul explain to us God's intentions for eliminating the age of the law. The law is where man did something for God. For thousands of years, man did all the work as we lived our lives with a dead spirit. We had to do good in our own power. We could only hear from God externally through prophets or miraculous signs. Man did not have the capacity to develop a personal, intimate relationship with God. Our spirits were dead.

However, through the death, burial, and resurrection of Christ, "you hath he quickened who were dead in trespasses and sins" (Ephesians 2:1). At that time, man was ushered into the implementation of the age of grace. The age of grace is where God does something for man. He now does the work for us! Now that the age of the law has been eliminated, we are no longer the worker; we are the manufactured product of the Worker! We are His workmanship created in Christ Jesus (Ephesians 2:10).

Romans 6 explains the elimination of the law. It is pictured through the crucifixion. In Romans 8, the Spirit enters to dwell within us, and the age of grace is illuminated. This is a visualization of our resurrection with Him. Neatly tucked between these two chapters is Romans 7. Here we see evidence of an internal battle within during the time that comes between our crucifixion and intended resurrection. It is the tomb time of revival! Revival does not take place on the cross or without the tomb. Revival takes place *inside* the tomb. The reason that the Saturday between Good Friday and Resurrection Sunday is such a boring day, metaphorically speaking, is because Jesus is often lying in the tomb alone! But the "day we lay" is crucial to *everything* that comes after the tomb. And if we are going to die with Christ as well as rise with Christ, then we must also be willing to spend time lying in the tomb with Christ.

Many Christians die, but before they can be resurrected, they get frustrated with the boredom of the tomb and go back to their old lifestyle. The tomb is a time of rest, not a time of wrest! When we fight this process and resurrect prematurely in our own power, then we have to repeat the process of dying all over again. Most Christians would rather be on their cross where there is so much attention, pity, and sorrow? Others prefer to be part of the resurrection celebration? Few would rather sit lonely in a dark and damp tomb. There is no "praise of man" in the tomb. It is easy to see why people are not interested in their time in the tomb. But, just as you do not die on the cross alone and you are not resurrected alone, Christ will not leave you lying in the tomb alone, either.

Look back to the prophecy of Hosea that we saw earlier and you will see this truth. "Come, and let us return unto the LORD: for he hath torn, and he will heal us; he hath smitten [the crucifixion], and he will bind us up. After two days will he revive us [revival]: in the third day he will raise us up [resurrection], and we shall live in his sight." We finish our time on the cross with Christ rather quickly. Likewise, we are resurrected with Christ in no time at all, but we had to spend *days* in the tomb in between!

How do we endure that? How do we get ourselves to rest with Him in that tomb? We enjoy the crucifixion, especially when our spirit is right. When we are frustrated or discouraged, we resist dying to self, but we have a longsuffering God. We do not know how long He will suffer, but we know that He is willing to suffer. Through preaching and discipleship as we walk with God, we experience the conviction of our sin, and that is when we eventually but willingly enter into our crucifixion. We recognize the joy that comes from a selfless crucifixion.

The saying "no" to self along with the sacrificing and the pain of crucifixion are given hope by the knowledge that we will soon resurrect. But, often as we sit idly by in the time between the crucifixion and His resurrection, we become somewhat dormant in our faith. We are bored with our lives, and we find ourselves stepping out of the tomb prematurely. Then, we begin to live our lives in our own power. Sure we are alive. We walked right out of that tomb. But we did not walk out with Him! As a result, we do not have Him living for us or working in us. We went from being His product to being man's performer! We will try things in our own power for a while and then find ourselves struggling again real soon.

This truth is clearly shown in chapter 26 of Isaiah. Here God tells us exactly the purpose of lying together "in state" with His dead body prior to the resurrection. "Thy dead men shall live, **together with my dead body shall they arise**. Awake and sing, **ye that dwell in dust**: for thy dew is as the dew of herbs, and the earth shall cast out the dead. Come, my people, **enter thou** into thy chambers, and **shut thy** doors about thee: **hide thyself** as it were for a little moment, until the indignation be overpast." (Is. 26:19-20)

Here we see that the tomb is a place of protection. It is not the place of crucifixion. It is not the place of resurrection. The tomb is the time in between the death and the resurrection where we can bypass His indignation for our failures. *Indignation* is the righteous anger of God. We experience great forgiveness when we are willing to crucify and lay in state. The tomb is the time when God's indignation turns from righteous anger toward forgiveness. Safety is found *in* the tomb. Isaiah starts verse twenty by saying, "Come." In order to enjoy the tomb as much as we enjoy the crucifixion or the resurrection, we must first come to Him.

Matthew 11:28 says, "Come unto me, all ye that labour." In the tomb, you cease from your own labor, because it is no longer you; it is Christ in you. It was an incredible burden to get on the cross. The cross is hard labor! That was true even for Christ who came into the world for that purpose. Likewise, it is an incredible burden to sacrifice our will and our desires and submit to dying daily.

But, before we can get to the point where we are ready to resurrect *with* Christ, we must get to the position where we no longer do the work *of* Christ, but where He does the work *for* us. We must progress spiritually from Romans 6 to Romans 8—but we have got to stop trying to get there by bypassing Romans 7. Many of us never reach the glorious *resurrected* life of Romans 8 because we do not want the battle for supremacy that takes place in the tomb of Romans 7. It is in the dark chambers of the tomb that we experience the complete dearth and death of our sinful soul. If both Lazarus and Jesus had to wait for their flesh to rot, so do we!

We looked at the first part of Matthew 11:28,

but the rest of the verse says, "Come unto me, all ye that labour and are heavy laden, and I will give you..." wrest? No! He gives rest! Is there a lot of rest on the cross? No, there is only pain on the cross. Is there a lot of rest in the resurrection? No, there is great work to be done as a result of the resurrection. So where is the rest? Our time in the tomb is our rest. We learn from our experience in the tomb that Christ intends to do all the work.

Now, please look at what Jesus said in the next verse. "Take my yoke upon you, and learn of me; for I am meek and lowly in heart: and ye shall find rest unto your souls." (Matt. 11:29) His yoke is his burden. His burden was his DBR. It is during the burial time that we learn from Him. In the tomb, it is just He and we. We are alone with Him in the sweet fellowship of Savior and student. Here is where we learn, and once we learn, we can rest with Him...for today we lay! It is our soul—our mind, will, and emotions—that must reject our tendency to work instead of find rest. To receive His rest, our soul itself must die to self and lie in state upon His shelf!

We say, "I struggle with wrong thoughts. I am negative, pessimistic, jealous, and angry. I have this stubborn habit, and I have this unfulfilled or insatiable addiction. I have to get it out. I have to stop, and it has to die." So, we conclude we must crucify these affections and lusts. We say "no" to that selfish appetite, and we experience our wonderful crucifixion. However, rather than going through the trial of the tomb, our soul (which so desperately desires to do that thing for which we just crucified ourselves) rejects the tomb time, where we would have found the rest we needed as well as God's power to do His great work.

God says, "I want your soul to rest. It is of no use to Me!" The Apostle Paul highlighted this truth when he wrote, "Glorify God in your body, and in your spirit **which are God's**" (I Corinthians 6:20). He says nothing about our soul. That is because we cannot make God look good in our soul because it is not His, it is ours. We can only glorify God with our body (how we look) and with our spirit (how we respond). That is God living through us.

We have to be willing to return to the tomb.

In Hosea 6, the prophet first said "come," and then he said "return." Many of us crucify ourselves and we get into the dark, damp dungeon of the tomb; but then we step out prematurely without realizing the protection from God's indignation was in that tomb. Now we must return. This protection from the elements of the enemy is the time we need to learn how to relax with Him. Then, we can emerge in His resurrection power. We have adequately learned to yield to Him.

Some think it is lonely in the tomb. But it's not! We are only cut off from contact with those around us. That is part of God's plan. Isaiah 55:6 says, "Seek ye the LORD while he may be found, call ye upon him while he is near:" He is near when we are in the tomb. When we are in the tomb, He is right there with us. We might say, "Oh, it is dark in here I need some light." But He will respond softly. "Shhh! Wait and rest." We need to remember we are in the tomb with Christ. We need to settle down and keep still. We will see Him in the tomb if we just do not prematurely pull away.

We get off of that cross, we go into the tomb, and we become bored. We think nothing is happening, and so we begin to make things happen in our own power. This is the exact mistake Abraham and Sarah made. God had promised a son to Abraham, but years had passed and nothing had happened. Humanly speaking, the situation was hopeless, so they took matters into their own hands. Abraham took Hagar, and she gave birth to Ishmael. How much of the pain and suffering in our world today is due to that one decision by Abraham to act prematurely in his own power rather than yield patiently in faith!

We prematurely reject the resurrection and leave the tomb, only to come face to face with our need to experience our crucifixion all over again. Many Christians are stuck in this reciprocal cycle. They are baptized into His death, but they are never raised to walk in newness of life. They just keep going from the crucifixion to the tomb and back again.

First, we need to come. Sometimes, we need to return. Finally, Hosea said, "After two days will he revive us." This is a metaphor. In our case, it may not mean a literal two days. It could be longer or shorter. But remember the period in the tomb took longer than the time on the cross. The period in the tomb took much longer than the resurrection. For multiple days, Jesus lay in the dark, boring dungeon of the tomb. "Then [after the tomb] shall we know, if we follow on to know the LORD:"

Matthew 16:24 says, "Then said Jesus unto his disciples, If any man will come after me, let him deny himself, and take up his cross, and follow me." Metaphorically speaking, Jesus Christ is saying, "If any man wants to have a life worth living, He is going to have to do what I am going to do. He is going to have to take up his cross, which means a sacrifice." Everybody is called on at times to sacrifice for the sins of another. We go through great turmoil in our lives because of the sins of other people. You might say, "Well you don't understand what my husband did to me" or "You don't know how my wife acted." May I remind you that Jesus understood what we did to

Him and willingly sacrificed anyway? We are going to have to sacrifice for the sins of others in order to take up our duty and follow Him.

I have found that there is great discouragement in the period of time between the crucifixion and the resurrection. But, when I am willing to endure that period of discouragement by sacrificing my selfishness and accepting the darkness of His passing indignation, then in the morning, I can come out of the tomb with Him in His Power rather than my own. If we come out of the tomb in our own power, there will be no Light. But, when we stay there as long as God requires, we will come out in the Light of the newness of life. For yesterday was the day I lay. But today, He might say, "Lazarus, arise!" Don't be lazy. Be Lazarus!

CHAPTER FOUR
TODAY? HURRAY!

PAUL'S DESIRE WAS TO BE FOUND IN CHRIST. To experience true freedom in our Christian life, it is not enough to be found with Him in us. We have to be found IN Him. Until we are in Him, we will remain bound to the power and passions of sin. Because of our stubborn refusal to develop intimacy with Christ, we fail to wholly give ourselves to the Holy Spirit. We may have Christ in us, but we are not living IN Christ. Think with me for a moment about the difference in those who are found and bound, and those who are found and unbound.

When our baby students in Reformers Unanimous are spiritually struggling for an extended length of time, they will inevitably return to their previous patterns of addiction. Though they *have* been found by Christ, they remain somewhat bound by sin. But I have found that the students who immediately develop their personal relationship with Jesus are found and more quickly *un*bound from their addictive behaviors! However, I also see Christians who have sat in our church pews for decades who are found and (seemingly) unbound, yet there is no spiritual growth! I often see more spiritual development in a sixteen-week old drug addict than in some church members' sixteen-year relationship with the Savior. I have seen more tears in a single local jail service than I have seen in all the Christian school chapels I have preached, combined! The spirit in our Christian schools is often like an anvil—cold, hard, and dark.

What causes such apathy? Why can new believers from the worst of situations grow bigger, faster and stronger than life-long and second or third generation church members? It is usually traceable to either the Christian's unwillingness to die to the socially acceptable desires of self or an unwillingness to rest in state for the resurrection with the Lord Jesus Christ. Many are just not willing to endure the apathy that comes from serving others. Because of this, they miss out on the power of His resurrection and struggle to get emotionally involved in the work of the Lord, as a result. When we do this, we become selfish Christians. Selfish Christians may not do bad things, but selfish Christians are usually bound to something that keeps them apathetic toward others.

The way Paul describes this process lets us know that there are two steps involved in enjoying the benefits of our sanctification. It is important to remember that justification is just one step—belief. Salvation is by grace through faith alone (Ephesians 2:8-9). Do not get justification and sanctification confused. I have never met a victorious Christian who was mixed up on this issue!

As we mentioned earlier, while justification and sanctification are immediate and instantaneous, enjoying the benefits of our sanctification is a process of progress. And if we do not take that second step of progress, we will never enjoy God's promised benefits of our sanctification.

A) The "Found yet Bound" Have Christ in Them.

When Christ comes to live withIN us, we receive the Holy Spirit. Colossians 1:26-27 says, "Even the mystery which hath been hid from ages and from generations, but now is made manifest to His saints: to whom God would make known what is the riches of the glory of this mystery among the Gentiles; which is **Christ in you, the hope of glory.**" We mentioned earlier that *hope* means expectation, and *glory* means to bring the right opinion. It literally means to make God look good. So here is what Colossians 1:26-27 is saying: "Having Christ IN us is the only expectation we have of making God look good."

This is the mystery of all ages: though we are fallen creatures, Christ, through the indwelling Holy Spirit, is going to live in us. And since the Spirit of God dwells *in* us, we are not **in** the flesh any longer. Now, at times, we can still walk *after* the flesh, but we no longer live our life *in* the flesh. That is the position of the unregenerate.

"...Now if any man **have not the Spirit** of Christ, **he is none of his**. And if Christ be in you, the body is dead..." (Romans 8:9-10). The body is "dead" because the body is where our sinful nature dwells. Sin brings death, but now as believers, we have the Spirit as our life because of His righteousness—it is not our life, but His!

The only way that anyone experiences a resurrection is by having the same Spirit that raised up Jesus from the dead dwelling in us. Jesus did not raise Himself from the dead, but the Spirit of God raised Jesus from the dead. Think about that. If we have the same Spirit who raised Jesus from the dead, don't you think we can have the same power with God that provided Jesus with power over man? Oh yes we can. That is God's design for our new life.

Having Christ in us is great! But having Christ come out of us is far better. Far too many believers settle for only having Christ in them. Their

Christian life seldom makes a difference in their relationships with others. There is a children's song that speaks against hiding our candle underneath a bushel. We teach kids that when we hide our candle we are not soul winning. But I know people who can win a thousand people to Christ on a doorstep, but they cannot win one person to Christ in their workplace. Why is that? It is because their spirit is hidden under the bushel of their outer man. As a result, anybody who knows them does not want what they have!

But I know other people who attract the lost. It seems as if everyone who comes to know them wants whatever it is that they have. That difference is found in the Power with God which manifests itself in great power with man. It comes from a man who is broken and spilled out. It comes from a man who is not hiding his Candle under his bushel. That expression literally means that the Spirit of God is making His way out of you and He is not being hindered by your flesh. You have died, patiently waited in state for your resurrection, and you look to Jesus on Resurrection Day and say, "Is it today?" "Hurrah!" is your response as He nods and rolls the stone away!

The purpose for adversity in our life is to cause the indwelling Spirit from within to permeate out of us. Adversity is intended by God to blow a hole in our soul so that the inner man may flow through. Yes, this is the purpose for God-ordained adversity: that we may be wounded through a crucifixion, so that He can permeate out of us through His resurrection. This is the crucified Christian life. It is not only Christ in you; it is you in Christ.

There are three reasons why believers are set apart for sacred use but may remain sacredly *un*used. First, some are not willing to get up on the cross. They are not willing to say, "Lord, crucify me." Then there are others who do go to the cross, but immediately get down as soon as they are scorned by those who are watching. These people are incapable of saying, "Father, forgive them." Finally, there are those who get into the tomb, but then they realize that they did all that sacrificing and nobody is noticing them anymore. They are not getting any attention for the sacrifice and the people for whom they sacrificed do not seem to appreciate it. So they get out of the tomb on their own and lose access to the resurrection power.

When we reject our tomb time, we lose our position with Christ. We lose that all-important affiliation that comes only when we exit the tomb together with Him. As a result, we experience our new death, but do not receive the joy that comes from the new life. I would not want to die every day, much less throughout the day all day, without getting a chance to resurrect with regularity.

When Christ is in us, we possess the Holy Spirit. But that does not mean that He possesses us! Look again at Philippians 3:9—"And be found **in him** (that is under His influence), not having **mine own righteousness**…" When we are not IN Him, we are forced to rely on our own righteousness. That is self-righteousness!

Righteousness has two meanings in the Scriptures. Each of the two meanings of righteousness is tied to one of the dual benefits of salvation. Again I say, at salvation, we experience justification and sanctification. These are two different simultaneous experiences. Justification is freedom from the *penalty* of sin. It means that we do not have to go to hell; we get to go to heaven. The other benefit is sanctification, which is emancipation from the *power* of sin. Sanctification means that sin no longer has dominion over us.

When it comes to justification (freedom from the penalty of sin), all my righteousness are as filthy rags. I cannot do anything to get to heaven; God has to do all the work. We all understand this truth. But I ask you, if God does all the work for justification, who does all the work for the righteousness of sanctification? God does. God does all the work to save me and He does all the work to change me!

When we are trying to do it all in our power, then that "try hard to do better" mentality steals our joy. Doing good in our own power is the actual definition of self-righteousness. It means that we have trained our soul—the mind, will, and emotions—to think good thoughts, to want good things in the will, and to feel that which is right. Then when we end up doing wrong anyway, we just get mad at ourselves! As a result, we live under constant condemnation.

Regardless of how hard we try, we cannot do the work of the Lord in our own power! If we are living under condemnation, it is a sign that we are not trusting God for our sanctification, but trying to work it out in our strength. That never works! We should remain in the tomb and wait for His prompting. We may ask, "today?" But if He is not moving toward the morning light, nor should we!

As we experience sanctification, we are empowered to be "more right on earth." All of the power for both justification and sanctification comes from the Holy Spirit. To experience that power, we have to develop an intimacy and a walk with God that will develop the inner man—that is our spirit communing with His Spirit within us. The inner man must be developed so that we can yearn, learn, and discern how to hear from Him. Only when we begin to do that can we begin to live under His power. Absent an intimate, personal walk with God, we will find ourselves living self-righteously.

Have you had the experience of moving into a new house and trying to get used to where everything is? When you have lived in a place for a while, you can get up in the middle of the night and navigate confidently, even in the darkness. But try that in a new home, and you are likely to end up with a broken toe or a bloody nose. The more you reside in a place, the closer you are to abiding in it.

Jesus told the disciples in John chapter 15 that unless we abide "in Him," then we can do nothing! Have you ever felt like that? Do you know the feeling that no matter how hard you try, you just cannot get the job done? But if we abide in Him, we can do everything. We must see how dependent our spiritual life is upon abiding in Christ. Abiding in Him is the only way in which we will bear fruit (John 15:5).

Lets take a moment and look at the fruit in our own life. Forget about looking at someone else's fruit (we all do far too much of that), and take a good, hard look at your own. Is there a disconnect between what we say about your abiding relationship and the fruit that is expected of us? If there is not "much fruit," either Jesus was a liar, or you are in denial about abiding in Him. Which is it?

I could tell you, "I am in Christ. I have been in Christ for fourteen years." But though I have been saved for a long time, I have not been living in Him for all of that time. There are some days when I have not abode in Christ for fourteen minutes! I want to be sure that you understand what I am saying here. I am not saying that Christ ever leaves us. He has promised never to do that. I am saying that we consistently resist His influence. If He goes forward and I go back, how can I say I remain in Him?

Have you heard that Baptists are sometimes called legalists? This is a foolish accusation. Legalism means that one gets to heaven by doing good works. Though we would like to reject the label, I am afraid that sometimes it fits better than we want to admit. It is not because we believe in legalistic justification; but rather it is because we often train our children to engage in legalistic sanctification. We know justification is all of God and nothing of us, but somehow, we believe that when it comes to doing the work of God (our role of sanctification), we have to do it in our own power. That is going back to living under the law. The law was intended to bring us to Christ because it makes us realize that the harder we try to be good, the more we realize we cannot do it!

When I came to Christ in 1993, I was a drug addict, alcoholic, and had other crippling habitual sins. But for the most part, I wasn't too bad of a guy. Today, I *think* I am a *worse* man than I thought I was back then. Now I am not saying that I am a worse man than I was back then, but that I think I am a worse man now than I *thought* I was back then. Why? Because the closer I get to Christ, the more I realize that I am continually falling short of who Christ intends for me to be.

That is the purpose of the law, our schoolmaster. It was to teach us that no matter how hard we try, in fact the harder we try, the more we are going to fail. I am not saying that there is never a need for us to try; I am just trying to tell you that we are not human *doings*; we are human *beings*. God did not tell us to "*do* ye holy." He said to "*be* ye holy." God does not want us to do something for Him; God wants to do something for *us*! He wants us to be something. Christ came not only to save us from sin's penalty, but to provide us emancipation from sin's power, as well. That emancipation is not the result of Christ in us; it is the benefit of us abiding in Him.

B) The Found and Unbound Live IN Christ

When we enter into Christ, not only do we have the Holy Spirit, the Holy Spirit should then have us, as well. The best description of "in Christ Jesus" is found in Romans 8:1—"There is therefore now no condemnation to them which are **in Christ Jesus**, who walk not after the flesh, but after the Spirit." This is the working definition of those who are IN Christ. They are those who do not walk after the flesh, but after the Spirit.

The flesh is your body's desire to lead your

soul. The flesh is satisfied by the soul's willingness to be under the influence of the body. All of us have outside pressure trying to negotiate with our heart to do exactly what our body wants. As we have already seen, that is where sin dwells, within the members of our body. At the same time, we have the Spirit of God dwelling in us saying, "No, go this direction." Our soul (which is where our freedom dwells) has a choice to yield to the Spirit and be under His influence, or to submit to the body's desires and be under the influence of the body.

When we walk after something, it means we are taking repeated steps in succession of that which we are following. When we are taking repeated steps after the flesh, we are walking after the flesh. But if we are walking after the Spirit, or in the Spirit, we are taking repeated steps after the Spirit. If we are IN Christ, we will say no to our flesh, and proceed in the direction of the Spirit. To walk that way is to repeatedly do so. When we do this, we will not live under condemnation.

But if we are walking after the flesh, then we are

not walking IN Christ. We are going to experience condemnation. But that condemnation is not going to come from God, it is going to come from Satan. I have to tell you that I have experienced this far too much in my life. Many people get confused because they do not understand the difference between condemnation and conviction. There is a difference between what conviction produces in us and how condemnation prosecutes us.

When we sin, conviction arrives to *convince* us that we can stop this wrong. Conviction is good for us, and we need to keep our hearts sensitive to it. Condemnation is different. It says, "You're never going to do anything for God. Look at you, you loser, you're a fake." That is not what the Spirit of God does. The Holy Spirit does not give us words of condemnation. He is an Encourager. He is the One saying, "You can do all things through Christ!" He wants us to have all of the best that God has for us. We will properly respond to the leading of the Holy Spirit if we will place ourselves under His magnifying glass.

But when we are out from underneath the

influence of the Spirit (though that does not necessarily mean we are living in wicked sin), then we are walking after the flesh. We do not always want to admit or recognize this, but good flesh is just as bad as bad flesh. We cannot please God, no matter how much good we do if we are in the flesh (Romans 8:8). Being self-righteous means that we are doing right; we are just doing it our self! That is what most of us prefer to, or unknowingly, do.

I have told our Reformers Unanimous students many times that smoking dope does not make one a bad Christian. Not yielding to God makes us a bad Christian. We stop yielding to God long before we engage in our addictive tendencies.

There are addicts with strongholds who are doing as good as some Christians who are in church every time the doors are open. Now do not misunderstand what I am saying. There is a big difference between unrighteousness and righteousness. Dope is unrighteousness, serving God in His power is righteousness. But what's in the middle? Our self-righteousness.

In Revelations 3:15-16, God said to the self-righteous crowd, "I know thy works, that thou art neither cold nor hot: I would thou wert cold or hot. So then because thou art lukewarm, and neither cold nor hot, I will spue thee out of my mouth." Why would He rather we be cold (unrighteous) than lukewarm (self-righteous)? Because it is easier to get a man to take a step from unrighteousness to righteousness than it is to get someone to take a step from self-righteousness to righteousness.

There are some Christians who occasionally engage in their addiction (and they are certainly not being righteous when they do that), but they are so shallow in their relationship with Christ that their only alternative to doing good in His power, is to do bad in their own power. They do not know how to do good in their own power yet. But give them time, and they will learn it just like we did! And then *that* will be their battle. Is that not what Paul said? "For that which I do I allow not: for what I would, that do I not; but what I hate, that do I" (Romans 7:15). If the Apostle Paul could not do the things he knew he was supposed to do, why are we even trying? Just stop trying so hard! Let God do the work.

As we continue our discussion on the difference between having Christ in you and you being in Christ, we need to return to Paul's teaching in Romans 8. "For the law (the rule of conduct) of the Spirit of life **IN Christ Jesus** has made me free" (Romans 8:2). That is a great description of being found and unbound. The word *free* describes the unbound life. Salvation made me free from the *law* of sin (sanctification) and death (justification). It is the law of the Spirit which is IN Christ Jesus that has made us free from the *power* of sin and death.

After Jesus raised Lazarus what did He say? "Loose him and let him go." (John 11:44) It really does no good for us to walk out of the tomb in our own power with the garments of the tomb still wrapped around us. Lazarus was alive, but he was still bound. So, Jesus commanded the people to loose him. Why? Because He cannot use us if we are still bound. The Spirit of life in Christ Jesus is that which makes us free from the law of sin and death. Lazarus was alive because of Christ, but He still needed Christ's help to be unbound.

The change agent that He gave us to do this great miracle is not ourselves. It is not a better me; it is a dead me! **Christ works best through the body of a dead man.** We die that Christ may live. We need to exercise the proper measure of faith to accept that. We need a measure of His faith to believe that there is an abundant life far better than the redundant life we have endured for so long.

In Galatians 3:1, Paul is writing to the church of Galatia, a church that was zealous of many good works. But they had been led astray into false doctrine. Paul said, "O foolish (ignorant) Galatians, who hath bewitched (charmed) you, that you should not obey the truth, before whose eyes Jesus Christ has been evidently set forth, crucified among you." They had been a zealous church, they had done many great works, but now they were no longer submitting to what they had personally and previously experienced. They had once experienced something unique and personal, and it was quite awesome. But they had ceased to submit to it, both individually and collectively.

Paul continues on in verse 2-3: "This only would I learn of you (that's like saying I've only got one question for you) received ye the Spirit by the works of the law (did you get saved by doing good works?)" That is a rhetorical question; both they and Paul knew they got saved by the hearing of faith. "Are you so foolish? (Are you so ignorant?) Having begun in the Spirit, are ye now made perfect by the flesh (in your own power)?"

Paul was asking them how, having had Christ begin the work for justification, they had come to believe they were able to do the work of sanctification in their own power. The church of Galatia was guilty of self-righteousness.

We need to understand that the chapter and verse divisions in the Bible were not in the original text. So Chapter 3 is not the beginning of a new section. The thoughts opening Chapter 3 go with the verses that end Chapter 2. And by looking at these verses together (chapter 2:20-21 with 3:1-2), we can see what caused the Galatians to cease to submit to what they had previously experienced.

In Galatians 2:21 Paul said, "I do not frustrate (I do not stunt; I do not make void) the grace of God." Paul declared to the Galatians that they were stunting the grace of God in their lives.

Again, grace is when God does something for us; the law is when we do something for God. I don't know about you, but I'm a pretty busy man. If God wants to do something for me, I sure don't mind if He goes ahead and does it! The church of Galatia stunted the grace of God and hindered what God intended to do *for* them. Then Paul went on to say, "for if righteousness come by the law, then Christ is dead in vain." Paul was saying, I do not stop God's work on my behalf, for if the ability to *get* right or the ability to *stay* right comes from me doing the work then Christ is dead in vain.

By relying on self-righteousness, the church at Galatia was stunting God's work and making the cross of Christ of no effect. Now I know I don't want to do that, and I am sure you don't either. So how do we avoid that? Go back one verse to verse twenty: "I am crucified **with** Christ;

nevertheless I live, yet not I, but Christ liveth in me. And the life that I now live in the flesh, I live by the faith **of** the Son of God."

Again we see that it is not our faith, it is His faith—the faith that He gives us when we accept Him as our personal Savior. We do not need more faith. We already have all the faith we need. We just have to be willing to yield to His confidence rather than our confidence in the face of adversity. In the face of adversity you say, "I need to respond right, but I can't." Yes you can! You can do all things through Christ (Philippians 4:13). You just have to believe.

I don't know how many times my wife and I have talked about our lives and rearing our children. In difficult times, we often come to this conclusion: we just can't do it. And then we remind ourselves that we can't, but He can. Even when we know that truth, we can sure wear ourselves out trying can't we? We must stop trying and let Him give us the power and enable us to do that which we're called to do.

It all comes down to this one old English

word *faith*, which is a modern English word for confidence or trust. *Faith* is the ability to have confidence or trust in something. To understand faith, we can do no better than to look at the Hall of Faith—Hebrews 11. We see that faith is defined as the substance of things hoped for (hope is a synonym for faith) and the evidence is things you cannot see yet. If you could see it, it would not be faith. So when you hope things will be right, but you cannot see that it is going to be okay, that is faith.

The author of Hebrews says in verse four: "By faith Abel offered." An offering is how Abel *worshiped* God. Abel's Old Testament sacrifice was a way of expressing his faith; it was an act of worship. Abel worshiped God and he obtained a good report that he was righteous in faith that was expressed through worship. I can find a lot of people who worship God to express their faith. That's the number one way most people express faith.

Next, we see in Hebrews 11:6, that Noah *worked* for God when he prepared an ark. It's much easier to find people who will worship God than it is to find people who will work for God. But you can still find people that will work for God. In fact, there are some people who would rather work for God than worship God. They're in the nursery; they're singing in the choir; they work their fingers to the bone. But like Martha, they miss out on the blessings of fellowship with the Lord. There are many people that will work for God, and there are many, many people who will worship God. But notice in Hebrews 11 that God did not say He was pleased with Abel's *worship* or Noah's *work*.

But in between verses four and six is the story of a little-known man that God said pleased Him. Who was it? A man by the name of Enoch. God talks about Abel's faith, how he worshiped. He talks about Enoch's faith and how it pleased Him, and He goes into great detail about Enoch's faith. Then he goes to Noah's faith and lists nineteen or so other men and women. In none of those other cases does God say that their faith pleased Him. He only said that about Enoch. What made Enoch different?

It is simple. Enoch *walked* with God. Hebrews 11:5 says, "By faith, Enoch ... had this testimony, that he **pleased** God." The Bible gives us just a brief mention of Enoch in Genesis chapter 5:23-24. "... Enoch **walked** with God: and he was not; for God took Him."

That's right, Abel *worshiped* God; Noah *worked* for God; but Enoch *walked* with God. And because Enoch walked with God, he had this testimony: that he pleased God. You can find a lot of people who will worship or work for God, but you will be hard-pressed to find as many people who will consistently walk with God.

Have you ever noticed that the first hour of the morning which we intend to give to God is the most embattled hour of the day? Why is that? It is not that we hate Bible reading; it is not that we hate Bible meditation; it is not that we hate prayer. We actually enjoy those things when we properly engage in them. Then why is it such a battle? Because the devil knows that if we walk with God, we exercise faith. That faith, like Enoch's faith, will please God. If we please God, it is proof we have faith. With faith, we will attain His righteousness. If we have His righteousness, we will hear from Him regularly. If we regularly hear from Him, we will crucify ourselves upon His request. If we crucify ourselves as requested, we will patiently wait in the tomb for the resurrection. If we patiently wait in the tomb for the resurrection, we will soon enjoy the power of His resurrection. We will say, "today?" And scream, "Hurray!" as we step out in victory over sin. Having this power of His resurrection, we will know Him on an intimate level and experience a more pure meditation. This will grant us an enormous power on our life to influence other people. It is no wonder that the devil works so hard to get in the way of our daily early morning walk with God!

Enoch's faith is described in the next verse Hebrews 11:6—"But without faith it is impossible to please him: for he that **cometh to God** must **believe that He is**, and that **he is a rewarder** of them that **diligently seek Him**." Allow me to take a moment to show you the measures of faith that Enoch had as God lays them out for us in this verse.

Enoch *came* to God. I know a lot of people who every time they have a problem in life, they come to God. Though they turn to God for help in their distress, this is not enough faith to save them. It is simply enough faith to believe that God can help them.

Enoch *believed* that He is God. Now God does not want us to get rid of the people who come without saving faith. Jesus said, "…him that cometh to me I will in no wise cast out" (John 6:37). As they keep coming to God, eventually they will believe in God and in Jesus Christ and Him crucified. At this point they have enough faith to save them. But it is not His faith. Their faith gives them the agent, the Holy Spirit, necessary for change. But there are two other measures of faith that they still need.

He believed that God rewards diligent seekers. Now this measure of faith is where most of us are. We see dedicated Christians around us being rewarded and recognize that God rewards diligent seekers. This is what I call *information observation.*

We see it, but we do not submit to it. Although we know God rewards diligent seekers, we still seek our own reward instead of seeking His.

We focus on our own plans, our own desires, and we reject the opportunity to be crucified for each and every thing that God reveals to us as hindering our personal walk — all those conveniences, those things that we count as our gain. Because those things are appealing to us, we continue to conceal ourselves from Him and find ourselves not willing to begin the pilgrimage. We know God rewards diligent seekers, but we just don't diligently seek— the cost is too high.

But eventually, if we are willing to develop spiritually, we will come to the point where we not only believe that He rewards diligent seekers, but as a result of that belief we say, "I'm throwing caution to the wind. *I'm going to diligently seek Him.*" Dr. Curtis Hutson left a secure job with the post office to take the pastorate of a church that was too small to support him and his family. He told his wife, "If I starve to death, tell the devil I was fasting!" He was willing to risk everything to diligently seek God.

If you seek Him with your whole heart, what will happen? You're going to find Him every time. Jeremiah 29:13 says, "And ye shall seek me, and find [me], when ye shall search for me with all your heart." It's guaranteed that God is waiting for you at the end of this measure of faith—the measure that turns observation into participation. This is where you get out of the ship and walk on the water. This is where no matter what kind of adversity is in your way or what kind of elements are against you, you do not begin to waver as a result, and you are not going to doubt!

When we diligently seek Him we find Him. You see, a person who has this measure of faith is truly walking with God. This is the person who is living with God. This is the person who is not just living with God, but also learning about God. This is a person who is living with Him, dying with Him, and patiently lying with Him, as well. This man will meet God's goal for us to walk with Him. This man will be answered when he questions the Lord with "today?" and be so fortunate as to respond, "Hurray!" Up from the grave *we* arose!

When we walk with Him, He will make us uncomfortable. When we become uncomfortable, His Spirit will come in and make us comfortable. Then as we continue to walk with Him, He'll take us to a new level. When we get to that new level, He'll introduce us to a new devil. When we face that new devil, we will be uncomfortable again, and then the Comforter will come again and empower us. When the Comforter empowers us, we get that internal persuasion to take another new level. The Christian life will not be an easy process. It will be a pilgrimage that will lead us to do the impossible through Him over and over again. But we will not do it *for* Christ, he will do it when we are IN Christ!

CHAPTER FIVE
EVALUATING YOUR DBR

I WANT TO CLOSE OUR BOOK BY GIVING US SOME VERY PRACTICAL HELPS TO GUIDE US THROUGH THE PROCESS OF EVALUATING OUR DBR. We must never forget that we have an enemy actively working to ruin our life. But we must also realize that our God is much greater. Recognizing and remember this fact will help us fight our battles in His strength, not in our own.

I will first share some characteristics of our journey so that we may determine where we are in the DBR process. Secondly, I will give you some personal characteristics that will help us recognize when our own personal and self-righteous character flaws are hindering our DBR process. I believe this will help us remain committed to being a daily dying believer that regularly resurrects in His power.

A) Characteristics of the Journey

I. We must always remember that our progress is *personal*. We cannot rely on anyone else for our personal walk with God. It is not our pastor's death, our Sunday school teacher's death, or our parents' death, but *our* death that must occur. Other people's DBR may challenge us into our own personal DBR, but it CANNOT be a substitute for our own death, burial and resurrection. We each must be willing to daily die with regularity throughout the day. We must be willing to be buried in the tomb with Christ and wait patiently for that intimate familiarity with Him to form, that we may resurrect with Him. This process must become intimately personal to *us*. Your DBR process may *not* end up being private, but it will always be personal!

2. Our progress must be *consistent*. Yesterday's death will not crucify today's passions. Yesterday's burial will not give us intimacy for today; and yesterday's resurrection will not give us His power today. When God fed the children of Israel with manna in the wilderness, they were not allowed to keep it overnight. They had to go out each morning (except for the Sabbath) and gather a new supply. In fact, when they tried to keep leftover manna, it "bred worms, and stank" (Exodus 16:20). We must have a refreshing DBR moment each and every day.

We will probably never have a day where we can avoid a painful, personal crucifixion. But rejoice, for it is followed by familiar intimacy and resurrection power if you remain consistent in your approach *with* Him.

3. Our DBR process must be *progressive*. A failure to progress to the next step in our DBR process will stunt our pilgrimage and hinder His resurrection power. We will find ourselves going part of the way, and then wanting to stop when things get difficult. God loves us too much to allow us to remain like we are. He wants us to become like His Son (Romans 8:29). It is a progressive process and we cannot skip steps. It is *not* good for us or those we love to short change the DBR process. It is beautiful in *its* time!

4. Finally, our progress is *informative*. This information when embraced will develop interpersonal maturity with Him. The key to our "interpersonal maturity" is a daily walk with God as Enoch had. Remember, we do not walk with God in the morning. If you are like me, in the morning, you are sitting in a lounge chair reading your Bible and praying. That is not our *walk with God*; that is our time of *talk* with God. We talk with God in the morning and He gives us clear communication in our prayer and journal time. And then, we take those repeated steps that were revealed in our talk time throughout the day. This internal persuasion of the developing Spirit within us is our walk with God. Walking with God is something we do all day. It's not just spending time in personal devotions. (However, I believe walking with God is 100% dependent on an early morning, somewhat uninterrupted talk time with Him. It sets your course for the day.)

Our talk with God is a **communication** stream with Christ which leads to an internal leading from God. As we begin to communicate with Christ each and every morning, he will eventually pass on to us an internal leading from God. This is called internal **persuasion**. This is our walk with God. This internal persuasion of God comes from Jesus through the Holy Spirit (John 16:13-14). As we begin to experience internal persuasion, God intends to grant us a better understanding of what it is that He is asking us to do. At first, He will often ask us to obey Him without delay or explanation. But as we submit to obey His internal leading, He will eventually begin to explain in our spirit why He asks us to do things. That is when understanding of our mind will become enlightened. In other words, we *know* things in our spirit, but we *understand* them in our mind.

To illustrate that principle, think about this. When did you know in your spirit that "children, obey your parents" was right? We knew it was right when we were a kid, but when did we understand it – when we had kids of your own! That is the process of going from a baby Christian to an adult Christian. We move from knowing things are right in our spirit (where knowledge is found) to understanding in our mind why they are right. This is called Holy Spirit **illumination**. This illumination comes from the familiarity of a relationship that is submissive to the unexplained leadings from Him. When we are obedient right away and without delay to our internal persuasion of the Holy Spirit, we become familiar with Him and He with us. This familiarity increases our communication and increased communication develops our illumination.

Illumination is then followed by **conviction**. After we experience consistent internal *persuasion,* we begin to have an understanding of God's leading. Now listen to me carefully, illumination is not necessarily a sign that we have God's power upon us. It is the goodness and grace of God that grants us illumination. We do not have to understand to obey! It does make things easier when we understand exactly why God is asking us to do something, but we ought to do right regardless of our lack of understanding.

Persuasion leads to illumination, illumination leads to the conviction and conviction is the voice that calls for a dying to self for the sake, or the sins, of others. This three-step process kick starts our DBR progress.

When His *communication* brings us the internal *persuasion* of *illumination* that is when we must step up and say, "Okay. I see my flaw in this area and I must submit to His call for my crucifixion." This process followed on a consistent basis is what will develop a close fellowship with Christ. That is called an **affiliation**.

As I told you earlier, our affiliation with Christ is where most of us fall short in our progress. We refuse to wait patiently for God's power. When we reject our wait, we often try to do it in our own power. We decide to cease something that is clearly wrong, and when we can't stop, we get frustrated and want to quit trying. That is because too many of us are getting off of the cross or not waiting long enough for the affiliation of the tomb. It is that tomb where we and Christ join together as our soul life permeates into Spirit life.

Our crucifixion with Him followed by our interactive affiliation within brings us His power to rise above all difficult circumstances. A willingness to engage in this process is evidence of a dynamic love relationship with Jesus Christ. That is our **personal relation**. It is that kind of personal relation Paul was referring to in Philippians 3:10 ("that I may know Him and the power of His resurrection"). The resurrection is a result of our intimate personal relationship with Christ. Lazarus was resurrected because Lazarus and Jesus were "close". When we have to die and wait for Him to show up, it makes Jesus weep too. *If* we're close!

This intimate relationship with Christ leads to a proper thinking in the situations of life. Remember that our goal (which was Paul's goal) is for the excellency of the knowledge of Jesus Christ. That goal is the purer heart that comes from a personal relationship with Jesus Christ. A pure heart grants us the purer meditations to think properly in temptation. Purer meditations are the ultimate goal of our DBR.

B) Character Traits to Overcome

In conclusion, below are the eight steps to the purer meditations that are supposed to come as a result of our sanctification. Each step lists a potential and most probable character weakness of the soul that, if it is not crucified, will stunt our growth and hinder the ability to change the way we think. Remember, if we never change the way we think, He is incapable of changing the way we act.

1. If we don't talk with God in **communication** most every morning, chances are it is because we are <u>lazy</u>. When it comes to most things, I am a hard, hard worker. But I fight laziness when it comes to my daily talk with God. I enjoy it, but Satan fights it! If we are lazy, we will never experience communication with God. But some people tell me, "Brother Steve, I get up every morning and I communicate with God, but I don't experience internal persuasion."

2. If we are *not* experiencing an internal

persuasion, it is probably because we are underline distracted. Many of us ask God to do something, and then we get all worked up about it rather than resting in faith that He will deal with the situation. We cannot receive internal persuasion if we are too busy being distracted by our outside pressures. Be still and know God! This persuasion brings us illumination.

3. If we are not experiencing **illumination**, it is probably because we are underline stubborn. God may be showing us things, but because we don't understand them, we refuse to do them. In cases like this, God is not going to bother illuminating us; He already knows our heart. God knows that because of our stubbornness, we are not going to obey Him unless He explains *everything*. God is the King—He doesn't owe us any explanation; we owe Him unequivocal obedience. Let's first obey, and learn some things later! Freedom comes from obedience. Obedience comes from a fear of the Lord, and the fear of the Lord comes from knowing Him. When we are illuminated, it will usually lead to a personal crucifixion.

4. If we are not accepting our **crucifixion**, it is likely because we are <u>selfish</u>. We are rejecting our death to self because we are not willing to sacrifice for the sins or sake of others. Don't get me wrong; every crucifixion I have made has personally helped me. But more often than not, God intends for me to help somebody else more than He intends for it to help me. It took me a long time to recognize this truth, but when I did, I was more willing to be crucified. I need to recognize that people need a break … from me! Accepting our role in living the perpetual crucified Christian life will bring us an intimate familiarity with Him. This produces an affiliation with Him.

5. If we are not experiencing an **affiliation** with Christ, we are probably a <u>resister</u>. A *resister* is the definition of the Old Testament word scorner. God tells us to rest in the tomb and wait for God's righteous indignation to pass. But we often want to rush things. If we resist His place in the tomb, we are not patiently waiting. When we resist, we miss out on the familiarity of affiliation that only comes as we wait. Don't wrest, rest! We *resist* because we choose to *exist*! Die and decay, for today we lay! If we will cooperate with Him, we will soon see ourselves resurrect in His Power.

6. If we are not experiencing His **resurrection**, we are probably being <u>uncooperative</u>. When we wait for our resurrection and exit the tomb with Christ, He is not going to idly stand by as we ponder our preferences in life. He will immediately lead and empower us to do the impossible. However, if this makes us uncomfortable, we may become somewhat timid. Our timidity may be endured by Him for a short time, but eventually, timidity is stupidity! We will become uncooperative with His new levels and be vulnerable to the new devils. This will lead us back to square one where we will need to crucify ourselves all over again. Reject this compromising, uncooperative spirit and seize the moment to do the impossible as you exit your tomb with Him. When we cooperate, we will know Him and the power of His resurrection! That is the premise for our personal relation.

7. If we are not enjoying a **personal relation**, it is probably because we are <u>unresponsive</u>. There is nothing worse than loving someone and not getting a return response from them. It is amazing to me that we can receive His power to do the impossible, yet when He expresses unselfish love in return, we are selfishly cold toward Him. It is not as if God needs us! God has *chosen* to love fallen man. Yet so many Christians are not enjoying an abiding love affair with Jesus Christ. We say, "Give me, give me, give me." But what kind of love is that? Where is our heart's desire for quality time with God? We are unresponsive to the One who loves us most. When we truly love Him, He will occupy our mind. He will be our heartfelt meditations.

8. If we are not experiencing that purer **meditation** that comes from our personal relation, it is likely that we have a <u>critical heart</u>. This is evident when we actively perceive wrong in the lives of others. If our focus is on the weaknesses of others, we cannot know intimacy with God. A critical heart cannot cast down every imagination that exalts itself above our personal relation (II Corinthians 10:5). That is why we must meditate on the Jesus (Him and His words to us)—so that when we get in a discouraging circumstance, we have the momentum of proper meditations to work in our favor. When we do not meditate on the right things, it negatively affects our every relationship, no matter how intimate it is.

So understanding this eight-step process to purer meditation and comparing them to our eight character weaknesses that can stunt this process, let me ask you a question. Why don't we cooperate more with Him? I believe it is because we are not *really* interested in the benefits of our sanctification. We are more willing to skip steps and just plug away in our own power. Too avoid this futility of life, we must come to the point where we realize that God offers more satisfaction than our efforts could ever provide. We need to believe Him enough to lay it all on the line. If we will go through the process of a personal DBR, it will regularly transform our developing walk with God. We will come to personally and intimately know the Lord Jesus Christ.

Someone said that the definition of insanity

is doing the same thing over and over again and expecting different results. Aren't we tired of struggling and failing in our own strength? The reason we <u>can't</u> get any satisfaction is because we <u>won't</u> get a hold or our sanctification! Get on up there with Jesus on the cross. Lie down with Him in your borrowed tomb. Then when you awaken in the Spirit and He rolls the stone away, walk in His power into your new life! Start today! The greatest adventure of your life is about to begin. It is a pilgrimage! When we truly know Him and His power flows through our life, the results are overwhelming! Be high and lifted up by the most high. For there ain't no high like the Most High.

Daniel 11:32 says that, "the people that do know their God shall be strong and do exploits." Know Him and let's be exploited!